the Path Unseen

JEWEL SWEENEY

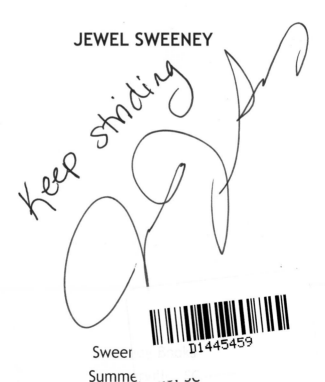

Keep striding

Sweer
Summe

© 2019 by Jewel Sweeney

Published by Sweeney Books

304 Foxglove Ave, Summerville, SC 29483

Printed in the United States of America

All rights reserved. No part of this publication may be reproduced, stored in a retrieval system, or transmitted in any form or by any means – for example, electronic, photocopy, and recording – without the written permission of the publisher. The only exception is brief quotations in the printed reviews.

ISBN 9781796926972

Scripture referenced from ESV The Holy Bible. Crossway Publishing Wheaton, IL ©2011

Other translations referenced are listed within text.

Psalm 77:19 - Your way was through the sea, your path through the great waters; yet your footprints were *unseen.*

Footprints

Chapter 1

Growing up, I become infatuated with the poem "Footprints." As a pre-teen, the concept was a great encouragement. The whole idea is that you are watching your life with God at your side as you walk. You hit the points of trials and tribulations and the pain is excruciating. Not only did you live those moments, but now you are reliving them. Then you look to the beach that you had been walking on and get a little upset. "Hey now, Lord. You said you'd be with me, but there's only one set of footprints." Isn't that just like us? We believe that good things happen because God is with us and that bad things happen because He left us. Facepalm. Then Jesus turns to the person and tells them, "It was in those times that I carried you."

Okay, so this whole poem creates a vivid world that we can picture. The poem is usually printed on a picture of a beach, right at the shoreline. As a child I loved this image. There was so much peace in knowing that God would carry me through the hard times. The problem was that I might have taken it too literally.

Scripture tells us, in those red words, that we will face trials and tribulations. There is no sugar coating. We have issues. We have problems. We must face them. It's easy to think we can just turn and run, but that isn't what Jesus wants from us. We cannot hit pause, hop on Jesus' back, then press play and allow him to carry us through the issues while we cover our ears and sing, "la, la, la," through the trials. However, when we stand and face our problems, He is with us. He does give us strength. We simply must stay in His presence. While in His presence, we can weather the storm of trials much better and, thus, we feel like He is carrying us through.

"Footprints" is a poem of great imagery. Perhaps this is one reason why I chose to stay close to the beach. During college, I often would go to the beach and walk along the tide. After a distance, I would turn and walk back towards where I'd laid my towel and books. Walking back I would search for my footprints in the sand. Obviously it was easier at the turn-around point as they were fresh. But then, either one of two things would become evident. One - the tide had come in and washed away the prints. Or two - the tide had receded and I walked with the tide, missing my tracks further up. Of course, there was also the possibility that someone had walked over them creating their own prints.

So often on those return-trip walks I would think about the old poem. I would think about the times that God had carried me through the wretched storms of life. As I would see the tide washing away footprints, toys, sand, and whatever else it could, I wondered if I too would have been washed away if God had not carried me.

But here I am, another decade older and still fascinated with footprints. Footprints tell where we have been. They show the path we've taken. Sometimes we look at our path and see only pains, heartaches, and mistakes. We can look back at all the harsh times and feel badly for ourselves. We can view it and see the growth we made. Positive or negative emotions can spur on greatness. Maybe the footprints are paths of greatness themselves. There may be footprints along a path we've taken more than once or new footprints and journeys with each step.

Paths are usually not in the direction we expect, or hope, or plan for. I have plenty of experience in this, as I'm sure you do too. For instance, this book. Better yet, any book I've written and published thus far. I am asked on a regular basis, "When did you know you wanted to become a writer." My answer stays steady. "Always."

As a child I loved to write. I would try my hand at journals and diaries. Heck, I kept track of my bowling scores when I was six. Writing was a true enjoyment. As I grew older, though, my validation came from sports, particularly basketball. By twelve, I had it all figured out: I need to become an all-star player, go to play at a Division I school, and go on to be a championship-winning coach. Once I accomplished those three things, I would write my journey and title the book, "From the Sidelines."

Well, I was an all-star high school athlete. I did play on a Division I college basketball team (as a walk-on). I went on to coach high school sports, as I hoped to. Then I left teaching and coaching to be a stay-at-home mom and a personal trainer. I thought that my dream of writing hit its end. After all, who wants to hear from a nobody? The footprints had all been washed away.

Little did I know, I had a story to write that needed more time. I owned a shop in Historic Downtown Summerville that allowed me the time I needed to write the story I had within me all along. It was a set of footprints I never thought I would walk.

Family changes caused me to close the shop and I continued my work as a personal trainer. Life was certainly different when I found myself writing stories for my kids- about my kids. After writing a series of six stories, I decided to seek publication. Now I have two published, one in the works, and nine more waiting in the wings.

Let me say this straight and clear: These footprints were not what I had planned. They were 100%, not even close to being on the radar of my life plan. (The books not the kids.) It was unseen and unknown. That is what this book is all about. Psalm 77:19 says, "Your way was through the sea, your path through the great waters; yet your footprints were unseen." So let's dive in.

Constant
Chapter 2

So Psalm 77 jumped off the page as I read it. Unfortunately, too often I get stuck in Psalms because I almost feel like they follow the same format. Many start with someone crying out to the Lord for help. Then we see praise to God for hearing and answering, or we see pain for not receiving the answer. Typically, the end is that God is still sovereign.

Don't get me wrong, I adore the book of Psalms. I need the repetition to get through my thick skull that God is sovereign whether something good has happened in my life or something bad. I find comfort in the words of David, Solomon, and Asaph as they cry out. I too need to cry out. I am not alone! There are many mornings that I don't feel very joyful and the chapter of Psalms I am reading is all about praising the Lord. Soon joy has caught from the words of the author into my spirit.

Psalmists didn't always create their songs from what was affecting them in that moment. There were many times that the psalmist was reflecting back past their own history to all of Israel's. This is the case with Psalm 77.

Asaph begins this song crying out to God, knowing he will be heard. He tells us that he is troubled, but that is a time to seek the Lord. He lets out a bit of what Jesus tells us- that when we cannot speak to God in our pain, the Holy Spirit will. Asaph begins to question if he has been forgotten by God. He wonders if God changed his mind about the Israelites and has decided to show no compassion. But through this meditation on the Lord, Asaph remembers. His memories don't go back to that summer he lost a job and God provided. No, Asaph decides to take it back to a nation's history of provision, and more – miracles.

Asaph decides to think about wonders, works, and mighty deeds. He thinks about - or is led in spirit- to the way God takes. The way of God is holy. Holiness means set apart. Thousands of years ago, people understood that God's way was different from every other way in the world. Yet here in the 21st century people say things like, "When is the church going to realize that times have changed?" as they wish for their pastor to marry them when he has set the rule that the engaged couple must not live together before marriage. Yes, times may be changing, but God is not. God's heart does not change. His holiness is still holy. He is set apart. We too must choose the path set apart from the times. Asaph saw this.

His searching for the Lord comes to rest on the holiness of God. He asks the question (v. 13) "What god is like our God?" His God has done great and mighty things. His God has rescued Israel time and time again. His God is different from all the other gods that are around him. This is the ultimate rally cry of a psalmist. Each god is supposed to have something to offer humanity. Our God offers a life set apart.

Asaph doesn't end with the realization that his God is greater than any god the neighbors and enemies of Israel can have. No, he goes to some of the best imagery you can find on the power of God himself. In verses 16-18, Asaph gives a picture we can all see and understand:

> When the waters saw you, O God, when the waters saw you, they were afraid; indeed the deep trembled. The clouds poured out water; the skies gave forth thunder; your arrows flashed on every side. The crash of your thunder was in the whirlwind; your lightnings lighted up the world; the earth trembled and shook.

Wow. Can we sit in these three verses for just a bit? Reread it over and over again until you find the little pieces of God that have been missed for generations.

Verse 16 says that the depths of the waters trembled. Think about what we find in the deepest parts of the oceans. So much is still left unexplored. But we know of amazing wildlife that is some of the deadliest known to man. The deepest parts of the ocean are home to scary, unknown, and unpredictable creatures, and it all trembles.

What an amazing word- *tremble*. When we first hear the word, we often think of fear. Have you ever been so scared that your body shakes uncontrollably? I think of two other times I tremble. My muscles often work to the point of fatigue, but before the muscles give out they tremble and shake. Weakness brings trembling. The depths of the ocean are weaker than our God! Man, does that fire me up. That brings me straight to the next time of trembling- adrenaline. We have learned that in times of panic or confrontation we choose fight or flight. It isn't done consciously. Our bodies are blessed with a pituitary gland that excretes adrenaline. From there the hormones decide what we are doing. Sometimes that frantic excitement or readiness to fight is bottled up within us. And you know what it does? It makes your body tremble. Do you think maybe the depths of the ocean see God and that reaction kicks in? Asaph says the oceans were afraid. But what about you and me? Do we tremble at the feet of God? Is it fear? Is it weakness? Or is it an adrenaline rush? The depths of the ocean fear God. Do we? Should we?

All the times we are told to fear the Lord, it is a different word than being afraid. Fear is reverence of God. Though the scariest parts of the world will fear the power and wrath of God, we can run into the safety of His arms. Do you not feel the protection of God from this verse alone?

Let's move to verse 17. As the depths of the ocean are trembling from fear of the Lord, the clouds pour out their rain. The skies thunder and arrows of God flash all around when God comes. In today's society we have come to see rain and storms as disastrous monstrosities. We wonder where God is. What if we stopped asking where God was during the storm and start acknowledging that He is right there? The rains fall because of God. Thunder and lightning are displays of his glory. The weather and climates, meteorology, is telling us of His presence. The storms are announcing his arrival!

You may have arguments about this idea. Sure a shower refreshes the land, especially in summer. And many people enjoy a lazy summer afternoon thunderstorm, the rumbles soothing them to a nap. However, others fear thunder. It shakes them at their core. The flashes of lightning causing trembling. And how often do those storms cause destruction along the land? The age old question arises: How does God allow bad things to happen to good people? Sounds like the beginning verses of this chapter to me. People cry out in a storm as Asaph does. But Asaph points out that the storms usher in the presence of God.

Verse 18 continues this theme. Asaph doesn't just say "the thunder and lightning". He says "your thunder" and "your lightning." How often do we think of thunder and lightning as God's? Perhaps we figure that thunder and lightning are God's when they mean punishment and wrath. Unfortunately, I think it's closer to when an older person tells the kids who are afraid of thunderstorms that the angels are just bowling.

Let's bring a concept and illustration from the New Testament to view this verse. Mary and Martha are hosting Jesus and his disciples for a meal. Martha is running around like a chicken with its head cut off to host. She's cooking, cleaning, setting the table all at the fastest speed she is capable of. In our terms, she's moving and shaking. Perhaps the weather feels this way with God. His presence causes the earth and atmosphere to move and shake.

Asaph is describing a storm that is rising because of God's walking near. Deep waters tremble. Clouds pour rain. Asaph says His thunder was in the whirlwind. I'm sorry, but this is a hurricane. As a born and bred northerner, I had little knowledge of hurricanes growing up. My freshman year of high school we tracked one in our Earth Science class. Since so few reached up all the way to Massachusetts with any force, our teacher thought this was a great assignment. The storm provided wind and rain, but nothing too terrible by the time it reached us. I didn't see the big deal. We battled snow and ice on a regular basis, so this seemed like nothing. Then I moved to South Carolina. I learned that hurricanes are so regular they have their own season. I learned they are so forceful they cause devastation. Reading Psalm 77:16-18, I see the storm described like a hurricane. Whirlwind, deep waters, rain, and trembling earth.

God's presence, His path, brought the nature He created into physical fear. And yet, He brought the thunder. He brought the lightning. Everything in this world is His. Or did we forget that? Thunder and lightning are like the horns being blown and the sentry calling, "Here comes the King!"

Have you ever witnessed the coming and going of major storms? I have. When the storm is about to hit, people come together. They help one another board up windows. They take down the outdoor furniture and store it for neighbors. It's funny, but people actually act like God's people. There is a lot more prayer as well. After the storm is the same. Prayer, selflessness, workers helping, and all the physical embodiment of Christianity. The biggest hurricanes produce the biggest acts of God's love.

Perhaps we need to see the storm for what it is- nature's response to seeing God.

Hippos
Chapter 3

Asaph's hurricane is not why you picked up this book. It isn't why I started writing it either. But I feel that in order to grasp the fullness of Psalm 77:19, we need to look at the whole psalm and this phrase of the song in particular.

As this storm is raging (because it saw God and feared), Asaph decides to switch things up.

"Your way was through the sea, your path through the great waters; yet your footprints were unseen." To really gather who God is, we watch a hurricane-type storm come to life when nature sees Him. Then, God makes His path straight through it. God's way is through the sea. His way is through the great waters. Let's unpack that.

I love hippopotamuses. Well, I've never been up close to one in the wild, so that may be why. However, a few years ago I was watching a show with my son and they gave an interesting, fun fact about hippos. Because hippos are so heavy, they walk on the bottom of the rivers and lakes to cross. They are capable of holding their breath for up to five minutes. So cool, but what does this have to do with anything?

God made the hippo as one of Earth's most dangerous animals. These animals are ruthless and insanely powerful. These animals weigh over a ton, so it isn't surprising they would walk along the bottom of the river rather than swim. But why create this creature to enjoy the water at all? That's a question you can ask God later. Me? I say it is another way to show God's power. Yes, the hippo is walking along the bottom, but it still needs to come up for air. Plus, this is fresh water territory.

In this verse, God doesn't walk along the bottom while the storm rages overhead. He doesn't rise to take a breath. No, our God is bigger than that. Asaph is trying to tell us that.

God walks through.

God walks through the sea.

God walks through great waters.

God walks through the trembling deep.

God walks through pouring rain, whirlwinds, thunder, lightning, and shaking earth.

My God walks through.

This series of verses brings forth the stability of God. Countless songs and poems have been written about the strength of God in storms being like an anchor. When waters rage against us, we hold on to him. Looking back at these verses I see why. We spent pages drawing the picture in our mind's eye of this storm Asaph describes. Here, God walks right through it and doesn't think twice.

God is choosing to walk through it all. I think it is important for us to see this. As humans, we often run from storms- literally and figuratively. Again as a South Carolinian, only 35 minutes from the beach, one is a part of a community that has evacuations for incoming hurricanes. We as humanity have seen the destruction that can come from storms and now know when to get out of the path of the storm.

This theory shows up in our emotional and spiritual storms. Many times we choose to evacuate from the incoming storms of our lives. Funny thing, though- in the past few years during hurricane season, it has looked as though my area was about to get pounded by a hurricane. Evacuations were not mandatory, but suggested. My husband and I would have people calling and texting encouraging us to leave. Each time we would watch forecasts and turn to prayer. Each storm I ask God, "Do we leave?" Not once yet have I heard, "Yes!" We've had storms without power. We've had storms with astounding wind. But we have not had the need to leave (yet). So often the places people suggested that we evacuate to get hit far worse than where we are.

My point? It would have been useless and more of a strain on us to evacuate. Our time, money, and sanity would have been wasted if we had followed the voice of man instead of the voice of God.

This is often true of emotional and spiritual storms that come our way. We look at the impending disasters coming our way and we run. We take off on the nearest evacuation route trying to escape the destruction when really, if we would just stay put, the storm would pass by with minimum damage. So often there is more damage done by running. The storm we think will hit actually hits harder where we run to.

When we see a storm coming, the only running we should be doing is to our prayer closet. We hardly ever think that walking through the storm is the answer. Yet there it is. God's path goes through the deepest part of the strongest currents of the ocean's storm. Why then does it not feel right? Sin.

Asaph's psalm begins with lamenting over God's hand leaving. When does God's hand leave us? Does He willy nilly change His mind? No. He repeatedly tells us that the only thing that keeps Him from us is our sin. That sin creates a false sense of peace in our lives. Are you getting where this is going?

Why do we fear God when it isn't the reverence term? When we are in sin. We fear consequences. We create our own storms. Then we run.

God walks through our storm, and every other storm. The path isn't the easiest. The path of God requires the most strength. Just like that hippo, the path requires a strength that others don't know.

Creating Storms
Chapter 4

The next question comes with self-evaluation. Are you creating the storms? As mentioned before, the storms came from being afraid of God. Are you acting in a way that is creating tumultuous surroundings?

The hardest part of our lives comes when we stop and look within. We must be completely honest with ourselves. Jesus spoke to the crowds in the Sermon on the Mount. In Matthew 7:1-6 Jesus speaks on judging others. Why? It is easy to find fault in others. It is easy to pick apart a person that isn't yourself. However, Jesus says,

> "How can you say to your brother, 'Let me take the speck out of your eye,' and behold, the log is in your own eye, and then you will see clearly to take the speck out of your brother's eye."

I don't believe that it is a purposeful hypocrisy. I think it's ignorance. It's pride, for sure, but we so often don't realize our pride.

Personally, I love this passage. It reminds me that many times I am picking at a speck of another because it split off from the log in my eye. What I dislike in other people is what I dislike in myself. That is usually true in everyone. Granted some things are just items we don't like in people, but typically if there is something I don't like about myself, I see it in other people so clearly.

Take some time over the next few days and look within yourself. Be honest with yourself. Find your sin. This isn't a witch hunt for all the things you don't like about yourself. This is an honest evaluation of what sin you have in your life.

There are two things you are going to need to do for this evaluation to work. First, open up the Bible. We should be in God's word daily. When we read the Bible every day, we know truth. In today's world I would guess that at least 75% of humans spend more time on social media than in the Bible. Think about the hours of your day. How many hours or minutes are you reading the Bible in a day? That can even include time during a church service if you need that to feel better. Now, let's figure out some social media. How often do you post? How often do you scroll? I know a good number of people that will take their phone into the

Hunker Down
Chapter 5

Hopefully by now, we all have searched within to figure out if the storm is coming from us or outside of us. If you have found some wave makers in your life, my hope is that you're in deep prayer and reading the Word. So now we have to look at the storms that rage around us.

There are going to be storms and raging seas because there is still sin. Sure, you're going with God, but sin still rages in the world. People and situations are going to come your way causing trouble and destruction the entire way.

It has been my experience that storms around us are actually good things. We are taught to see them as bad omens. We covered that they show us how God is near. (I think it is beneficial, still to look at a book from my favorite author- C.S. Lewis.) In his book, *The Screwtape Letters*, two demons are discussing the plan of action to take down a human. The supervisor is displeased that the human has to come to know Jesus, but he suggests making life difficult for that person. At one point the letters discuss that being apathetic is the best thing for them with the human subject.

When we are actively walking with God, we are powerful people. Powerful enough to walk through storms. If we choose a route that isn't God's it isn't always a complete loss. We may end up fighting unnecessary battles. But unless we are purposefully fighting against God, there is a good chance that at some point we will realize how to get through the storm and align with God.

People, possibly you, that have no direction, no fire, no desire to move, are people that are and will be the most useless for the kingdom. You might argue and say that it is those that are fighting against it, but no. Jesus tells us that being lukewarm is far worse than being hot or cold.

The ones that claim Jesus and let life happen without taking action hurt the kingdom. What they say to the world is that Jesus is fine, but we can keep living our lives the same way over and over again.

You may find my logic wavering, but let me give a vague example. I grew up in the north. People there are not in a fight against Jesus (as many here in the south believe). However, they are into their thing whether it is education, sports, politics, etc. If they find Jesus like my family, they need to own it. They are into Jesus. Many times, in my personal walk, was forced to defend my faith. Churches are not missing up north. Hear me in this, churches are alive and well. I don't know why there is this divide, but it exists, and for those in similar upbringings as my own, our faith is made our own in defending it.

For some reason, churches are more available here in the south. Because these buildings line street corners, it is more accepted that people will go to church. It is more accepted in the "Bible Belt" that people will "like" Jesus. I went from a liberal, public high school that emphasized the education of the person (not the test) to a liberal arts Baptist university that emphasized education in the Christian environment. I went from defending my faith to drowning in Christianity. Many of my friends were growing deep in their walk with God, but a teammate had stated what so much of the south was like, "We're all Christians here."

Over ten plus years in the south, I have seen so many people that live in their parents' faith and not their own. Don't get me wrong, this happens all over the country, but when it is easily accepted to like Jesus, it is more prevalent. These people- regardless of their zip code - do less for the kingdom than those that don't believe.

As storms rage on around us, we can easily choose to not walk through. It is less of a hassle to sit in a boat and let the waves move about us. Yes, we might get seasick, but we did a lot less work than we would by going through. So many believers choose this path as theirs. Then they just cannot figure out why they never feel right in church or around other believers. But still, that would mean that the storm came to us.

I love knowing a storm has come my way. I did not always. I felt continually that God was kicking me while I was down. I tried my best to live a godly life and it would be one thing after another. I would cry out to God (like the beginning of this psalm) and feel abandoned. Then I had my "*Screwtape Letters*" moment.

Satan doesn't send a storm to those that hang out in the boat, rolling with the waves. No, he brings the storm to those that are already walking with God. He wants to knock you off course. When we become so focused on the storm around us we don't worry about the way of God. The storm is the ultimate distraction from whatever our path before us.

These days, when storms arise I praise God. It is in these storms that I see the outside, sinful world is stirred and fearful because I am bringing in the presence of God. Satan is trying to take me out, or at least push me around some. If he and his demons can distract me from the path God has me on, maybe he can gain some traction in my life. If he wiggles in with hurricane force winds than maybe my relationships will also be in the whirlwind. What might happen to my marriage, my kids, my parenting, and my friendships? Remember what we went over in Chapter 2- the storm is a response to the presence of God. So we do make a little bit of our "outside of us" storms. We bear the image of God. Our surroundings will be afraid.

This may scare you a bit to think that the same Satan we read about in the Bible is trying to attack you. I only have one answer- this is why we put on the armor of God! Just yesterday I had a talk with my son. He was back to waking up in the middle of the night and, in his fear, he would wake up the rest of the house. He just finished a study for kids on the armor of God and I told him we needed to make sure that he was putting on the armor before bed.

You see, my son has had spiritual attacks during the night since he was two. I know God spoke to me while he was in the womb and said, "He will do great things." From that day on, I have held on to that truth and raised him (knowing and) instilling that truth in him. When the dreams began, we knew. I explained yesterday that if he is being woken up in the middle of the night it fits right into a battle to take out the whole family. Little sleep for him equals a whiny, fussy child nobody likes. Little sleep for dad equals a man with less patience. Little sleep for mom equals a walking nightmare for all. If we let the devil win, we hurt each other. As we put it all together my son says, "That sounds like an actual battle." I did not respond with "Duh!" like I wanted to. I simply said, "It is."

So often we think of the words of the Bible as imagery. We keep missing the facts of it all. It is an actual battle! Some of us are okay putting on the shoes of peace, helmet of salvation, breast plate of righteousness, and belt of truth. However, people are forgetting to hold up the shield of faith. We leave it at our side. Defend those blows of the storm with your shield. Then fight back. We hold the sword of the Spirit like it's an accessory. It's our offense! It will cut through the winds that try to damage us.

Look at the storm around you and see the truth. You have walked with God and scared those in sin. You are scaring Satan. Walk through that storm ready for an actual battle. And smile.

Philippians 3:20- For our citizenship is in heaven, from which also we eagerly wait for a Savior, the Lord Jesus Christ.

Isaiah 8:17- And I will wait for the Lord who is hiding His face from the house of Jacob; I will even look eagerly for Him.

I think Isaiah 8:17 is my favorite verse in this slew about waiting. It isn't just sitting and waiting. It is searching for Him. That is what the path of God is all about. It is unseen and we need to be the ones searching Him out. Many times our not yet comes because we aren't eagerly looking for Him.

Have you ever played hide and seek with a three year old? At first they sit where you've left them. Then they call for you. Over and over again. When you don't come out they begin the seek portion of the game. If they don't find you after a few minutes, panic will set in. Your child will either become more frantic searching under every pillow and behind every door or they will freeze. They give up. We sit behind the chair or stand in the bathtub while our child gets scared in the middle of the living room.

I think you see where this is going. Too often we pray for God to rescue us from the storm and when he doesn't come out right away we check the sanctuaries, Bible studies and pray again. After our go-to's, many times,

~ 37 ~

we freeze. When my kids would panic and they would keep searching, I would make a small noise that they would hear and get closer and closer. When they froze I would wait. When we keep searching, God keeps dropping hints to where he is. When we freeze, we usually stay alone.

Isaiah says it better than I ever could. We need our rescuer to come out. We await his arrival. When he doesn't come, even when he hides, we need to go on the hunt. He doesn't say, "I went to the temple last month." No Isaiah looked eagerly. He goes out with expectancy to find God and rest in the fact that God is the fortress to run to.

Scripture shows us that storms make us stronger, bring us to God, teach us to wait, and give God the glory. He is the only one who can walk through the hurricane we face. If we are feeling the shudders of demons, we are on the right path.

Shaking

Chapter 7

Sometimes we begin to enter life with Jesus and start out alright. Other times the storms begin immediately. Either way, if we are walking with God we know the storms will surge. Our reactions within storms will guide us either to God's footprints or away from them.

Psalm 55:22 says "Cast your burden upon the Lord and He will sustain you; He will never allow the righteous to be shaken." After I close my eyes and smile, knowing that my feeble mind takes in only a fraction of my God, I fumble my way through the pieces of this verse.

Cast your burden upon the Lord sounds like 1 Peter 2:5. Clearly this verse influenced Peter enough for him to repeat it. We say it all the time to ourselves and others, but it still takes some work. I think sometimes we feel our issues are too big to give up. Even though we know our God is big enough to handle them, we orbit around our problems rather than releasing them to God above. When we do this we have the ability to turn our problems into idols. If we don't think our problems are too big, we believe our problems are too small. We believe our God is so big that we and our problems are too insignificant for him to care for. We both devalue ourselves and demote God's creation. No matter the situation, we have made less of who God is and what He does for us.

The reason we cast our cares on God is because He sustains us. It goes back to *Footprints*. He is carrying us through the burdens. I like to look at it from the eyes of parenthood. My kids go through hard times. When they come to me and discuss it, I do what I need to do to help them. I carry them and sustain them as needed. Yes, my kids mess up, but when they do I evaluate the next steps to take. Sometimes they will need discipline, and they end up in a storm. Other times I will clean up whatever mess they've caused. Still, there will be times when I need to own. But no matter what's happening, I am there for them. I can guide and navigate them through. They can come to me for support. If I can sustain my children, how much more can God sustain us through our storms?

The second half of Psalm 55:22 truly ties in with Psalm 77 - "He will never allow the righteous to be shaken." When we are crying out to God in the midst of raging waters we shouldn't feel the shaking and rocking of the waves. We all know that feeling. We know when someone or something has gotten us off kilter. When life has decided that things were going too well for us that the monkey wrench needed to be thrown into the gears. Yes, those times we feel the ground move beneath us are scary. That's the point that the devil wants to make with us. He wants us to be scared. Fear takes our eyes off of God. Yet here we see that God won't allow us to be shaken. This makes me once again think of Peter. He had the faith to follow Jesus out on the water. But once the fear overcame his sight of Jesus, he sank. But Jesus didn't just let him drown. Jesus picked him back up.

There is a piece to that puzzle that I have been leaving out. Did you catch it? It isn't that God doesn't allow for anyone to not be shaken. God won't allow the *righteous* to be shaken. Some of you are really excited while others are now in dread.

Those who did not rejoice in that are thinking, "Well, I'm not righteous so I'll be shaken." Perhaps there was a particular time in our life that just flooded our memory. You might feel that it is obvious you are not righteous because of a time when you were so deeply shaken. I get it. I understand completely. I can remember feeling so knocked off guard that I thought the world would topple over onto me. Times that I was the one being wronged. I felt hopeless. But when the dust cleared, I realized that I was okay. Life was alright. Well, things were hard, but I was on solid ground. My emotions created hard rain and wind. The environment was a hurricane, but God did not let it shake me off the rock.

It isn't because I'm right and perfect. Not even close. However, we have learned that our righteousness is not our own, but of God. Over and over in God's word we see that those who are righteous are those that believe and follow God. So apply this to Psalm 77. We follow God in our path. We believe and gain His righteousness- we cannot have our own because of sin - and then we will not be shaken.

What an amazing promise we are given. I just want to sit in it. God sustains us. And because of His son taking our sin, we are granted righteousness that keeps us stable through the storms. Just one piece of that will make me smile and relax in His love. And we get it all.

If you're wondering which path is the one you should be on, I would ask you this: Are you shaking? Are you on solid ground or is it moving you all around? Right there you should know whether things are going in the right direction for you or not. It isn't that our path is easy, or takes a straight line, but our path will experience hardships either way we go. If our footing is sure and we are not shaken it is a good sign we are walking in the right direction.

If you can't make life work day to day without being shaken, perhaps it's time to rely on the only righteousness that is true. So often we assume that we are the ones in the right place, but there is nothing that we could do to earn our own righteousness. Romans 3:10 tells us that "There is no one righteous. No, not one." It is only by the grace of God and his love for us that we can achieve righteousness. When we refocus our hearts on Him, things will change. Place your trust in him and allow him to sustain you.

Learning what God's sustenance and stabilization feels like takes time. We learn to hear only his voice and feel His hand. As we continue to grow in Him, we learn how to follow Him through the raging waters of the storm. It's how we are able to know His steps.

Unknown
Chapter 8

The first thing that catches my eye in Psalm 77:19 is the last line. Asaph has called to God to remember Him. He describes the storm he is facing. Then he states, "Yet your footsteps are unseen." My first thought was quite sarcastic. "Obviously, Asaph. How do you see footprints in the water?" There was a little note above unseen. I got excited. Yes! A better explanation. "Hebrew: original is 'unknown'." Unbelievable. That's it? *Unseen* is really translated as unknown. How does that help me?

That's when God smacked me upside the head and said, "Let's see what happens." He sent me on the journey of writing this book. My eyes were opened to insights that needed to be shared. All the while God was whispering the way.

Have you ever been in one of those lazy rivers they have at water parks? The fake tide pulls you around as you

lounge in a tube. There's something fur
going through the river. The problem
long time to get the tube to get in the
to be a popular attraction. I've been
for people waiting to get in. When someone ו...
tube, everyone is eager to grab it. While waiting for the
chance to get in, or helping a child into a tube, one can feel
the current pulling them away. The path is predetermined.
Everyone follows that current.

Compare that river to the ocean. I'm sure most of
you have been to a beach and waded in the water. If there is
a strong rip current you may not even be allowed in the
water, but to a designated point. I have spent many beach
trips marking where my things were left before heading to
the water. Even the slightest current will take a decent
swimmer with it. When two currents meet, they can pull
someone out to the ocean quickly and dangerously. It's a
much swifter current than a lazy river.

When God walks through a hurricane, he creates his
own current. It might be exciting and revitalizing. It might
be scary and a rush. Depending on where we are with our
relationship with God, how we feel that current will change.
There will be moments that we feel the refreshing water on
our feet, the current pushing us, and we will be looking for
the first tube to hop in and ride along. Other times when
God's current comes by us, we panic. We swim back to

quickly as we can without wanting to be brought deeper waters.

In general, the current will be scary. It takes us through storms that we can see and bigger storms we don't know exist. We won't be able to see where we're going, but we can feel. Whether it is a lazy river or an ocean's tide, we know what fighting a current feels like. It can take our feet out from under us without the slightest heads up. When we know the current's direction and force we have a better chance of navigating with the current rather than fighting it. We can grab the tube and float along, but we have to be in tune with the current.

Learning the feel of God's wake is a necessity for navigation. Sometimes He doesn't take the most direct route. If you don't believe me, check out the path the Israelites took from Egypt to the promise land. It makes me think of some cartoon or comedy that shows a bunch of loops on a pirate map crossing over and back until they reach the 'x'. God does not say following Him will be rainbows and jellybeans. Things will get tough, but He is there to carry you when you need Him. The thing about the Israelites' path is that it could have been more direct. But when Moses sent the twelve spies, ten forgot that God was leading. Their fear kept Israel out of the promise land and into a longer journey than necessary. God was walking through those scary waters and the Israelites weren't used to his leadership. They didn't feel where He was going.

This isn't something crazy to learn. I was once told that my conscience was the Holy Spirit. I accepted it at the time, but have always struggled with it. Let's face the facts. The conscience tells us the difference between right and wrong. People do bad things and know that it is wrong. They just do not care. I would like to expand upon what I was told and say that the Holy Spirit works in us to move us to doing what is right. Being honest, there are many that do what is right, but don't know God.

What does this have to do with feeling God's path? So often people put the words Holy Spirit and feelings together as emotions are feelings. That isn't the case. The Bible tells us that we are prompted by the Holy Spirit. As a mother, I get this. When my children were little (or if they lose their mind or manners) I would hold whatever it was that they asked me for until they said "thank you." I didn't even get what it was that they wanted unless they said "please." Over time, the manners they were taught went from repetition- "say please" - to prompting. Eventually, less and less prompting needs to be done. As my children grow and learn what I expect of them, they will automatically do what is expected.

That is the process we go through as children of God. We learn how to speak to God. We learn what he expects of us. We know before we do it if it is what He wants us to do. And if we don't know, we ask with our best manners, so to speak. And just like our kids grow up and we require more of them, the same is true for us as we grow in the Lord. Also, it requires us to spend time with him. Prayer and reading the Bible help us grow and learn his ways. As that happens, the promptings of the Holy Spirit might change as well. We go from things like, "Don't flip off the guy that cut you off," to "Go speak to that woman. She needs someone." Unfortunately, that is where we start, isn't it? It is God giving us nudges in the arena of "don't do" first because we have to leave our sinful desires. You may notice that not all sinful issues will leave us quickly. This is where the devil will try to shake us. See, the Holy Spirit will prompt us to go and minister to someone or lead a Bible study or start a ministry. Then in comes one of Satan's goons to remind you of your sin. You become lied to and taught to believe you have to pass those sins to do God's work. Do you feel the waves?

It makes it hard to follow God through the hurricanes when we don't know how to grasp the promptings of the Holy Spirit as our path. Reading the Bible will open up a map. Praise and prayer show the legend. Obedience gives us the route to take. It is highly important to take the path that God has for you. If I wake up tomorrow and decide that writing and speaking may be what God has told me to do, but that I'm going to devote myself to my physical training and get on some TV show to show Jesus to a different and larger group, there's a good chance that bad things will happen. I'm guessing the ultimate failure will be me. I can even try to alter the smaller path and have failure. For instance, I love to write chick-flick style novels, straight Hallmark Channel style. After writing a couple and sending them out, I have had only rejections. And yet today, I have had no concern for them. I love writing them. I enjoy it. However, I don't think that is the path God has for me. Instead I am diligently writing this through headaches, fogginess, and leg pain. God is giving this work inspiration and life. All I can do is reach for the hem of His garments and listen to the promptings of the Holy Spirit.

Faith
Chapter 9

I love diving into God's word like this. It seems the further you dig, the more God reveals to you outside of the passage. I'm awed by this simple truth of God walking through the storms around us. It doesn't faze him for a second. Why should it? He's God. But it still makes me stop and absorb.

Further into Psalms, Ethan the Ezrahite has his turn to bring praise. In the 89th chapter of Psalms he begins singing of the love of the Lord. He gets into a new verse in the song and uses words we might just understand.

"You rule the raging of the sea; when its waves rise, you still them."

During our journey through Psalm 77 we have yet to really focus on why God walks through this storm without an ounce of trepidation. He rules the raging sea. The waves have no authority or power over him. We know it, but do we let it sink in? Does it permeate our minds and souls?

By now you may be like many Christians I know. You might be saying, "This is all well and good, but I'm a New Testament Christian. I need New Testament words to live by." First let me say, I'm sorry you feel that way. I too need words from the New Testament, but I'm not limited to them. Many words spoken in the gospels were based upon the Old Testament. Christ spoke to the people using what they knew; their traditions, their experiences. It took many who knew the Old Testament to understand what was unfolding within their lives that is becoming, as we know it, the New Testament. I encourage you to read the Old Testament to understand the New Testament. For far too many years I only dabbled in reading the Old Testament until one day I said, "No more!" And my eyes were opened by seeing the New Testament fulfilling Old Testament promises.

But for those that need a taste from the New Testament here it is. As Ethan says, God rules the raging seas. The gospels give an account of Jesus in a boat with the disciples. Jesus has been preaching and ministering, making him quite tired. So what does he do? He takes a nap. We've been there. The gentle rocking motion puts us to sleep. The exhaustion of the day takes over and he lets himself rest. I know that feeling. One long day after another leads to the physical crash. Our Lord shows that. Then he shows that it's okay to rest. I love this visual, but that's not why we're here.

Jesus falls asleep on a boat. He falls asleep on a boat with a group of fishermen. The fishing crew begins to worry because a storm starts brewing. Jesus, the carpenter, is asleep, but the people that make a living on the water are in fear. Isn't that how it is with us? A storm comes in the vocation we have and we panic. Then, when Jesus isn't joining us in our meltdown we do what the disciples did-wake him up. With him rolling eyes, sitting up, we think, "Now we'll know what to do." And here is the Lord's response to the storm around us: *Be still*. No, not to us, to the wind.

In three gospels we see that Jesus controls the storm. The wind and rain cease immediately. Many people might think this was probably just some little breeze and rain. Possibly, this was a coincidence. But studies have shown that where they were, stuck in a valley between hills brought great winds and wind tunnel like effects, and the storms could spring up so quickly and violently that those fishermen had every right to be scared. But storms on the sea don't dissipate in a snap. Not unless Jesus tells them to. Let's look at our three accounts.

Matthew 8:26- And He said to them, "Why are you afraid, O you of little faith?" Then He rose and rebuked the winds and the sea, and there was a great calm.

Mark 4:39- And he awoke and rebuked the wind and said to the sea, "Peace! Be still!" And the wind ceased and there was great calm. He said to them, "Why are you so afraid? Have you still no faith?"

Luke 8:24- And they went and woke him saying, "Master, master, we are perishing!" And he awoke and rebuked the wind and the raging waves, and they ceased, and there was calm. He said to them, "Where is your faith?"

Each of these accounts has slight variations to details, but not in ways that change the story. The first part of the storm is the wind. The wind causes waves that force water into the boat. The disciples are scared of the storm, but they're agitated with Jesus. If you have never experienced this in your life I would wonder what your life is like. In their frustration, the disciples wake Jesus up. In all three, it is stated, or screamed, by the disciples that they are perishing. However, I like Mark's way the best. The disciples ask Jesus, "Don't you care that we are perishing?" I have been there. God, don't you care about me? Don't you care that I'm depressed? Don't you care that my job is killing me? My debt is killing me? My family is suffocating me?

But, Jesus is not worried by the waves coming over the boat. He stands up and tells the storm exactly who is in charge. What has he to fear? God created wind and rain for good. Satan decides to use it for evil. Then we get a brilliant reminder that everyone and everything is under the subjectivity of Jesus. One day every knee will bow on earth and under the earth and declare that Jesus is King.

Why is the path we need to take through the seas with raging storms? So that Jesus can calm the storm. The world needs to see and know the power of Jesus. Sometimes people need a storm or two that only Jesus can speak to for them to see and know that power. And when the power of Christ takes over and the storm ends, others around us see the end. Going through the storm brings glory to God again and again because only he can tell the storm to be still.

When we look at these three gospels as they tell Jesus' defeat of the storm, they all say the same thing. Jesus looks at his disciples and asks them where their faith is. Those words hold true more and more don't they? The disciples were told to have faith in the midst of a terrible storm. I like to imagine that Satan was in the midst of that storm. Can you imagine if the storm had won? The boat topples and Jesus drowns. Now the Messiah has lost and all of the disciples are either drowned as well, or hopeless. Maybe Satan though he could tempt Jesus into using some other methods, but here it is. Jesus calms the storm with his words - because everything is subject to his authority - and instead of giving the devil a lick of anything, he turns it on his disciples. Where was their faith that he would prevail? He called them out, point blank- your faith was not on me, but on your life ending. Here we are, thousands of years later. We have storms rising around us. We follow Jesus through with all of our fears and doubts and he still turns to us and asks the same of us. "Why are you afraid? Where is your faith?" Personally, when I know this I feel a little better. If those that were physically in the boat with him didn't have enough faith, my lack of faith seems more manageable.

The key to faith rings true. Whether our faith is bigger than the storm or smaller than the fish we catch in the boat, Jesus conquers the storm. We can look at the storm as Satan trying to drown us or our hope, (or!) We can see each storm as God showing us he is always in control.

Footwear
Chapter 10

As we continue to look at this passage, I see the physical. During a writing course I took years ago, the instructor informed me that I had strength in detail only when it came to the physical. We don't need to discuss my weaknesses - there are too many. But my specialty has always been in bodies. I was an athlete from childhood through college. I am a certified personal trainer. Anatomy and Physiology are not just easy courses, but enjoyable parts of everyday life.

So when I go back to Psalm 77:19- "Your ways are through the sea, your path through the great waters; yet our footsteps were unseen," I think of God literally walking through the water. I don't see God running. I don't picture Him power walking. Instead, I see calm and collected God walking with dignity through the ocean. We too should be this calm as we follow Him through the waters. Why so?

Ephesians 6 gives an amazing depiction of a soldier readying himself for battle. The third item he puts on is his shoes. Those shoes have one name, but a varying layout depending on the translation of Bible you use. Verse 15 says:

> "and having shod your feet with the preparation of the gospel of peace;" (NASB and KJV)

> "and put shoes on your feet so that you are ready to spread the good news of peace." (CEB)

> "and, as shoes for your feet, having put on the readiness given by the gospel of peace." (ESV)

> "and with our feet fitted with the readiness that comes from the gospel of peace." (NIV)

> "for shoes, put on the peace that comes from the Good News so that you will be fully prepared." (NLT)

Over and over we are told to put on shoes of peace. Why would peace go on our feet? Why is not peace associated with the breastplate where our hearts are? I've questioned these pieces of armor countless times over the years. It hasn't been until studying Psalm 77 that I saw why.

We are looking for the path that God has designed just for us. Let's be honest, we would like an easy path, but that is not what we have been told we will get. And the closer to God we get, the harder it gets. Our steps must be covered in peace. If we cover our steps in panic, life will get more turbulent.

When we see these shoes of peace to walk in, we must know where the peace comes from. Peace comes from the gospel. The gospel is the Good News. Again, the good news is that Jesus has already taken the victory. The war is already won. Oh, WE of little faith. In the big picture and grand scheme of life we are worried over little things. All the while, Jesus has defeated death. And he did it all for us; the faithless worriers.

For me, the rest of the shoe part has the greatest impact. Whether it is said before or after due to translation does not matter a bit. What matters is that we put on shoes that are wrapped up in peace for readiness! We need peace if we are to be prepared. Prepared for what? Battle! The storms that come and try to sweep us away! Moving!

When we look at the armor of God we see one tool for the offensive - the sword of truth. We find four items of defense - helmet, breast plate, belt, and shield. Those shoes? They are defensive for sure. We dodge and slide evading the attack of the devil. I always believed they fell into only that category. But then God opened my eyes to see the truth.

prepares us, that peace, is not our own. Galatians ⌐
specific about the fruit of the spirit. Peace is a part of t
fruit of the spirit. We cannot have substantial, transcending
human understanding peace if it comes of ourselves. That's
why I say go back to the basics. Go back to who and what
started you on this journey that made you care where God
was going. Then you and the Holy Spirit can have it out.
You will rest in his peace and not your own. That is where
your boldness will come from. Your readiness can only
come from above. It is then that we will see the path to take.

Peace Out
Chapter 11

The path around the storm is usually more appealing to our senses. We see that wide is path that leads to destruction. Wide and easy. Heck, just as the after school specials would say, "Everybody's doing it." That is, after all, some of the draw to it. If so many could take the path, why couldn't I? Well, because, we have been told not to take it. Our path is the narrow difficult path, one must be surefooted. But in order to walk our path, sometimes we must be the ones that make some waves.

Previously in this book we discussed that storms can come from us in our sin or outside of ourselves with others wanting us to lose our way. Now that we've looked at so many other aspects to understanding Psalm 77, I want to look at an unpopular concept. There are many times that we are so focused on having a life calm that we will avoid any ripple of unrest. But if we look to the beatitudes in Matthew, Jesus says, "Blessed are the peace makers for they will be called sons of God."

I have a friend that will talk about this verse to literally anyone. The main point is that it says peacemakers, not peacekeepers. We can keep peace day after day after day. And you know what? It will crush our souls if we do it long enough. We enter into situations around us every day where we have to make the choice to keep the peace or make the peace. It's often harder to be a peacemaker if you are like me, nonconfrontational. People, when they first meet me, assume that I will toe the line with anyone. Truth be told, I hate addressing anyone in confrontation.

Just recently I had a tent at a market that was near children. I have no quorum with children in general. If I have an issue with a child it is more likely that I have the real issue with their parent(s). After all, a child doesn't know the level of their obnoxiousness unless the parent has taught them appropriately. However, at this market, vendors' children were playing in every area they deemed valid. One child decided to throw fits on my table. Another child wanted to shake my tent at his will. I asked each to stop. The tent shaking child then though it was okay to hide from his friends under my table with a floor length table cloth. Look, proper manners say you don't allow your child to hide under tables of people you have never met before.

So again I spoke to the child, asking him not to hide under my table. He seemed terribly offended by this. And between my agitation of screaming children being rude and parents not disciplining, my nerves were starting to get the better of me. After confronting the child I was officially stressed. The next day I had another market and another inappropriate child. This one was two though, and not well watched. The child left her mother's table and walked between me and mine. I attempted to speak to her and got nothing. The mother didn't notice until the child had stomped on my foot on her way past. I was agitated. The mother's response? "My child." Not once was there an apology for her child, just acknowledgement that her child shouldn't have done that. My response? I complained to others.

In one scenario, I did what I could to make peace in my situation. The confrontation originally caused me to stress. I waited for the mother to come and say something to me. But as time went on, I had no issues. Not only did the mother not approach me, the child stopped messing with my things. In the other scenario I kept the peace. I didn't confront the child or parent. Peace was kept in the market, but not in my soul. I was agitated and frustrated. I entered my nephew's birthday party complaining about this woman. That led to complaints from the day before. Unrest followed me around because I didn't make peace.

These are just silly examples, but I think they make the point. Making peace will have a time of storms for you and the other(s) involved, but there will come peace that is lasting. Keeping peace means that the storms will always be waiting in the wings. So often keeping the peace will mean an unnerving calm for the times when you are in the situation and violent lashings afterwards. Making peace means creating waves in that moment, so the peace can come after.

We always hear about the calm before the storm. It is often used more for relational times than meteorology. A toddler napping, for many, means calm. The toddler wakes up, storm. But the phrase began from weather and so we shall return to it now. Again, living in a hurricane prone area, I have been witness to this pre-storm calm. As many humans debate the go and stay, the animals have their radars going off. The burrowing animals burrow. The flying animals take flight. I love to go outside before the storm starts and listen to the quiet. But just as the calm happens before the storm, calm comes after the storm. Sometimes I feel like this is a Disney princess movie. The storm rolls through and pushes on. A day or more will bring back the animals and we hear the chirping, see the rabbits, and life is back in full force. Before we start singing with the birds, that calm can be more still than the calm before the storm. Sure we're all out milling about. We search for destruction. We wonder what we will find and we speak with neighbors in a way that is truly caring. The quiet and peace that come are more powerful to our soul because the anxiety of the storm is over. The winds have died down. The rains have ceased. The clouds dissipate or move along. The deep sigh of relief is released.

That deep sigh of relief comes after we make peace in our lives. But the sigh of relief happens in our spirits. Let's go back to Matthew 5. When we make peace, we are called sons of God! That means we enter the presence of Jesus! I love math. The associative and communitive properties allow for something great to be seen. Sons of God make peace. Therefore, Jesus makes peace. He didn't keep the peace when he entered the temple to find the money changers and greed. No! He made peace by making a whip, turning tables, and causing a scene. Think of the storm that made. I always try to picture myself as a disciple during those hours Jesus is making a whip. What do I do? Do I try to settle him down? Do I ask the men to clear out before Jesus can get to them? Maybe I take a nap or head home. After he makes a scene, what would I do? Do I apologize for Him? Never. Do I sit in shock? Probably. Can you imagine being a first-hand witness to the first and foremost peacemaker? We are too often worried about keeping the peace in the room that we don't know how to make peace.

The path of God stirs waters to the point of storms. The storm has potential for destruction, hurt feelings, damaged relationships, and lost friendships. But if there is peace that needs to be made, God might be asking you to make it. It will be difficult, but the end result is peace.

Now previously we discussed that a storm might be coming from outside of ourselves. Too often we get wrapped up in the fact that there is a storm, that we don't gather the facts. Perhaps this storm brought on by others is their response to God's call for peacemakers. We know that we are not perfect. But it is one thing when we see our imperfections compared to when another points it out to us it is hard to be humble enough to hear our faults, and to see that we have now played a part in this storm. It goes back to our self-examination, but also factors in the mindset that there are others like us wanting to be known as sons of God.

So don't hesitate to make peace in your world. There will be some high winds and raging seas, but peace will come after. Your path might require you to make the waves you walk through.

Optometry
Chapter 12

So in all of this, we still haven't touched on the big issue- "Yet your footprints were unseen." When I read this the first time, I thought Asaph was a little off his rocker. Come on. Obviously we won't see footsteps. We're in the water! I love walking along the shore, I love watching my footsteps get washed away with the tide. I've been in water so clear that I could see the color of my nail polish on my toes, but I never saw my steps. So why write this? Why make this part of the praise you are leading the choir singers in?

I think Paul gave the Corinthian church the answer, and I believe this entered into the canonization of what we call the Bible because its necessity. 2 Corinthians 5:7 says, "For we live by faith, not by sight." If you have been in a church for any number of months I'm sure you have heard this from the pulpit. Even if there wasn't a reference given, or if the sermon wasn't on faith, this has probably come up. We need it to be repeated to us though.

If we are doing life the right way, we will face hardships. Sometimes it seems like there isn't a light at the end of the tunnel. Dark moments will enter our lives in a variety of ways. Each person will eventually have to face a time where all they have is faith. (Let me just add to this: If you have not had a moment in your life that has required complete surrender to your faith in God, what He can do and what He will do, I would begin considering the notion that you do not have a healthy relationship with God. Think back to *The Screwtape Letters*.) For all of us who have been through this, we need to take a moment and look back at that time.

You may be in that situation now. For me, each book I write is an act of faith. Quite often I begin a book at the prompting of the Holy Spirit and know that I only have enough for a couple of chapters. I start writing thinking about how great an idea it is. Then as chapter three comes together, doubt sets in. Maybe this isn't supposed to be a book. Maybe I should do this in a blog series. What was a clear calm sea begins to become a series of waves with strong wind. Why? My path becomes unseen. I followed God into the depths of the sea and the nervousness sets in. In the grand scheme of life, this nervousness is mere potatoes. If God calls me to write, I write. If for some reasons my faith wavers, one of two things will happen. Either God and I will struggle over it as I run away and write new pieces or someone else will write it. It's that second one that motivates me some days. When God calls you to do something, He chose you to be in that path at that time for a reason. Who are we to stop? Why would we want someone else to do our job?

So we say it again - we walk by faith, not by sight. I think an interesting visual for this is Peter, Jesus and a boat. The disciples get into a boat and head off to the next destination. Jesus says something like, "I'll meet up with you in a bit." Matthew 14:22-33 tells the account. They set sail and get out into open waters when someone sees an apparition. Now, let's break some of this down a little further. Jesus sends away the crowd. Then he hits the mountain to pray alone. The boat is getting pounded by wind. Between three and six in the morning, the disciples see a ghost. Why do they automatically go to a ghost? They just saw Jesus perform a miracle and yet this certainly can't be him. I'm sure the disciples are exhausted. In addition to the "following Jesus" work, they also distributed food to over 5,000 people. Then they collected the leftovers. That's a good bit of walking. The disciples are in the boat, but it isn't smooth sailing. They have to fight wind, again. Sore muscles. Tired eyes. Here comes someone, it must be a ghost.

I get it. Just recently I did an east coast excursion. I took my children and drove up to Massachusetts on a Friday and back Monday night. The pre-dawn period is always the worst. It reminds me the day has ended and still I haven't slept. For many people the sky lightening would make things better. Not me. It makes me sleepy. I drove at this time and continually thought I saw animals just crossing the street. (That is when I found a truck stop to rest.) So I can completely understand why the disciples think they are seeing a ghost. They even scream in fear.

That's when Jesus says it's him. And here comes Peter. Mr. Spoke Too Soon Too Often. "Lord, if it's you, tell me to come to you on the water" (verse 28). At this point I believe Peter to be naive. Clearly he must be an only child. Because in my family, the person would tell you to come if you were going to embarrass or hurt yourself in some way, shape, or form. Well, Peter is trusting and I'm cynical. So Jesus says come and Peter steps out of the boat. Some may argue this as walking in sight not faith because he can see Jesus walking on the water. To that I would ask how often you walk on the water.

So let's continue on in this passage. The wind picks up again- those distractions as always. Peter takes his eyes off of Jesus to check the wind and he sinks. Fear beat faith. Jesus even says it in verse 31, "You of little faith. Why did you doubt?" It is an act of faith for Peter to walk on the water. He believes that Jesus will keep him up despite the fact that he has never done it before. If Jesus can break apart bread and fish turning it into a meal for thousands, he can walk on water.

We walk by faith, not by sight. Peter's sight was on Jesus. No, we don't have the tangible Jesus with us right now, but we know how to see Him. We know how to keep our eyes on Him. When we do that we can walk through the waters, not seeing our steps, and know that we're okay. We are going to be walking into unknowns all the time. We can plan each moment to the best of our abilities, but it still doesn't mean anything. The wind can rise at any moment to knock us off course. If we can walk in faith, it doesn't matter how strong the wind is, we will walk. When we walk by sight we will easily become distracted. And soon, we're drowning calling out for help. "Lord, save us." He does. His continual grace grabs us in the depths and pulls us out. And every time he asks us why we doubted. What is our answer? Fear? Insecurity? Hurt? Time and time again we will be given the chance to get out of the boat and walk on the waves. I hope we have the faith to get out, walk, and focus on Jesus.

Lighthouse
Chapter 13

It is a difficult process to walk on a path where we don't know where to go. And the footsteps we are to walk in are unseen. It's as if someone is against us. Oh wait, someone is! How can we possibly navigate the waves and storms to follow through the depths of the sea? It's the same way the ocean liners keep from the rocks and shores. Though these ships look to a lighthouse, we use only a light.

> Isaiah 9:2 - The people who walk in darkness will see a great light; Those who live in a dark land, The light will shine on them.

Now, I've read through Isaiah before and know that he was a prophet that told it like it was. He was humble and willing. He experienced God in an encounter that would scare me terribly. Yet he was bold and strong. So when I read this verse and knew that it needed a place in this book,

I wanted to fact check. The last thing I want is to take a verse out of context for the sake of a chapter.

So Isaiah has been discussing Jesus a good deal. We know the savior is coming. We know he will cause many to stumble within the Judaic community. And just before 9:2, we see He comes from Galilee. Immediately following we are told a light will be seen by those in darkness. The light will shine on people on dark land. At first this verse brought some fear to my mind. Light shining through darkness means revealing the sin. So the sinners will be receiving light. Wait? What? He's coming to be a light, but to all nations. That's the Jews and the gentiles. This isn't the end of times version of Jesus who is bringing judgment. This is the Jesus that was here to save the world. This light was one set on the land to guide people. The darkness in this sense is not our sin, but our lack of a way out.

During the ups and downs of kings for Israel, a lot of things changed. Some kings followed God and fought against the idols and small gods of their age. Others did what was evil in the sight of God. The prophets did their best with the wrong they saw. They spoke on God's behalf, often while the religious leaders turned their backs on God's laws. Throughout the tumultuous times, God finds the sacrifices repulsive. And He then begins to tell the world the only sacrifice that He will find acceptable - Jesus.

Thus, Isaiah talks of Jesus coming as the one who will be the sacrifice.

This is Jesus coming and saying, "I will show you how to walk." He is the only person that has gone through everything he did with the grace, humility, and everything else we don't always have. Jesus stepped down to this darkened planet to be the light. He guides us through the dark nights and cloud covered days.

It's funny that I think of going to the beach. When I go in the water, I make sure to make a mental picture of where my things are on the sand. I'm sure you've been there. Are you near a guard station? Is there a house or private entrance nearby? That type of thing. Why do we do this? Either someone taught us to do it when we were younger or we learned the hard way. The current will pull us as we go through the waves. The longer we splash around, the further we go. Next thing we know, we're a half a mile away from where we entered the water. We walk up to the sand and begin heading back towards our things in the opposite direction of the current. Sometimes that mental picture serves us well, other times not so much. I can be honest enough to say I have walked past my things before. The mental picture changed. When I showed up and put my things down, it was open and clear. As I walked back, crowds of people joined in the beach community and I completely missed my things. I've also messed up the other way! I was looking for the party of ten that I was about fifteen feet from. They all left. I thought it could have been the area but didn't see them. Wow.

Now, if only I had a large beacon where my things were. If something showed me more clearly where to walk back to, I wouldn't have missed it. That's why God gave us his son on earth. He knew that if we were to walk the right way we would end up in the seas where the currents would push us around. We need a light to see through the storm. Sure, the current moved us south, but we keep walking on towards the light knowing that the light is in the right direction even when it seems precarious.

How do we know the light will bring refuge? Psalm 119:105. It says, "Thy word is a lamp unto our feet and a light to our path." I have had this verse committed to memory since childhood. Back in those days about 95% of Christian songs came straight from scripture and repeated it over and over again. Even now as I write it, I sing the praise song. But it wasn't until adulthood that I truly began to understand it. You may be thinking, "It's pretty simple. What could you miss?" Let me share what I missed.

"Thy word" seems pretty self explanatory. Bible. Check. Next! Let's pump the breaks on that. We know that God's word is the Bible, but do we stop to think about the other meaning of God's word?

John 1:1- In the beginning was the word and the word was with God and the word was God.

Jesus is the human depiction of the word. So let's put that back into Psalm 119. Jesus is a lamp unto my feet and a light to my path. Puts Isaiah 9:2 into perspective, doesn't it?

Now growing up I didn't understand why biblical authors would repeat themselves so much. Something like this, as a child, would make me go, "Okay, I got it. Read the Bible and know where to go." I didn't understand the concept that repetition meant importance. So fast forward and I thought, "Ah, I need the word for certain. He is exclaiming importance." Oh the proud adolescent. Read it again if you have to. The two parts of that single verse are not the same.

We need a lamp at our feet. It isn't just to look down and make sure we don't step on a snake. No, this lamp illuminates our feet. It shows us where we are. Right then and there, when we dive into Jesus and who HE is, we are shown where we are. It may show us in a dark alley that we shouldn't be in. It may show us crowding in around others. Perhaps in a group going the wrong way or maybe hiding amongst other believers trying to live within their faith. Whatever it is, Jesus happily shows us. It isn't vicious or nasty condemning. Think of those office lights. Nobody looks or feels their best in harsh lighting. Jesus knows this. He is a lamp. Soft, gentle light. He needs us to look around and see where we are. How many times have you heard, "You don't know how far you've come until you see where you have been."? It's similar to that. We look to where we are. We take in all that's around us. Then we step.

We can't just step out off a cliff. God is not in the game of destroying our lives once we find them. There's part two. Jesus lights our path. We have a path lit up for us. I think anyone that has slammed their knee or stubbed their toe on a piece of furniture in the dark knows how necessary light is. I truly believe this is the God given example. Why? I have been to a variety of places in my life - different cities, different businesses, and different homes. You know what I don't do in new places? Walk around in the dark. Walking in the dark of some new area for me would surely end up with me getting hurt, getting in trouble, or doing something stupid. However, when I am in my own home, I know the layout. I know where doors and furniture are. Yet, I forget that I moved a shelf, table, box, what have you, and now I'm in pain. It was my pride in my own knowledge that kept me from turning on a light.

When it comes to walking on God's path, the lamp and light are always on. Our pride cannot turn of the light of our path, but it can try to block it. When we set aside our pride we are able to walk a well lit path.

So here is Jesus. He shows us where we are and then shows where to step next. If we were left to do it on our own, we would keep hitting our shins on the coffee table of life and likely quit.

How grateful we should be for Isaiah's prophesy! Jesus came down to light up the world. We navigate through the stormy waters with our eyes on the light.

Big Feet
Chapter 14

Recently, I took my children up to Massachusetts. This was a big adventure for the two young South Carolinian natives. Over and over I was forced to listen to the excited little ones that were ready to play in the snow, as the trip was scheduled for February. They have had the chance to catch flurries and had one snow storm accumulation of eight inches or so. I remember just how many times the kids came in to warm up before heading back out. I knew that they were just thinking of snowmen.

I tried to ease the thrill by telling them there was no guarantee of snow just because it was winter. There was a good chance of week old, brown snow, but not fresh snow. They didn't care. And to their delight there was about six inches of accumulated snow on the ground at my family's home where we were staying. We arrived Friday night in exhaustion. Saturday morning I heard little else than, "Can

Who is that?
Chapter 15

There is an interesting point with Psalm 77 that may be missed. As mentioned, it is written by Asaph. Most of the psalms are written by David. We see David grow up through the book of Psalms. Little by little. There are his praises from boyhood; I like to think he learned those from Jesse. Then life moves forward. He is anointed king. We watch as he goes into hiding. We see him cry for his life. Most of our favorite psalms are those written by David. Then we have a few by these people whose names we don't know or have never seen. Asaph is one of those people that just fly past us on the page as we read.

Over the last decade and more, reading the Bible is more than just seeing the words on the page for me. I want to know more. I believe this is where we should be. Yes we know a piece here or there, but what else? Cross referencing and diving into commentaries is my Biblical nerdiness. So when I see something like this psalm that intrigues me so, I want to know - Who is Asaph? Where did he come from? Why is his praise and wisdom placed within the canonical Psalms? So I dug a bit.

Asaph was a priest. That seems about right. So what? Well, he was not just hanging out in the temple singing. I mean, I'm sure he did that from time to time, but that wasn't only it. He was placed over the temple singers. Now you may be where I was on this, or perhaps you have more Old Testament temple livelihood knowledge. Either way, we should think on this a bit.

I grew up in New Jersey and Massachusetts before moving to South Carolina. In New Jersey, I was accustomed to seeing those in the Jewish community walking to and from the local temple on Saturdays. I've always been thankful for that exposure. My parents were quick and willing to explain it to me. Their Sabbath was Saturday, so they went to temple on Saturday. Why walk? Driving is considered work. Outside of that fact, I didn't ask much else and pretty much left it alone. Then I moved to Massachusetts at the age of eight. The state is predominantly Catholic. So I learned about CCD and Mass and other items of Catholicism. I had few friends of the Jewish faith, though I did get to witness a bat mitzvah of a friend. I watched as she recited prayers and sang. That was my only time in a temple.

After high school I entered the Bible belt. I attended a Southern Baptist university and the religious diversity dropped yet again. The Jewish community is less visible in the south than my childhood states. I stopped learning Jewish customs unless they were directly stated in scriptures, but, even still, others are stated in a way that is expected of us to know - because the Jews would know. As my faith grew and I began to read more and more, I realized it was my job to start figuring out these mysteries in black and white - or red and white. In small increments I began taking in more and learning more of the Jewish community. After all, we need to know our roots to know where and how our branches can, will, and should grow.

You would think that growing up in the church I would have put two and two together but I didn't. Maybe part of it was that I didn't care to put things together. Perhaps part of my lack of knowledge is Satan keeping us so focused on ourselves that we forget to look in other directions. At this point it is moot.

When I was a child, the churches I attended had choirs and a director. Through my teenage years, the shifts began, and praise and worship teams began the takeover. I never thought of the origin of it all more than just tradition. But even in the early days of "organized religion" we have temple choirs. I know that what happened in the temple is laid out and I could dive in to temple habits during the time of King David, yet, I still imagine a group of men standing in a corner doing monk-like chants. My mind is too small to grasp it all.

There in the temple was indeed a choir. The choir was chosen, as they are representing God's work and leading the Israelites in their songs to God. So often when I think of the priests, I picture a handful of men- descendents of Levi- that handle the sacrifices. I picture them burning the bull after slaughtering it just right. I see them entering the holy of holies with a rope tied around them and a bell, fear and wonder taking turns as facial expressions reflect their heads and hearts. I am envisioning (as feeble and incorrectly as it may be) a choir. I can hear harmonies echoing through the temple in praise to God. What must it have been like? All of the descriptions for the size of the temple are given. Now I can't help but believe that part of the design was to encourage acoustics. We've all done it at some point- We know which bathroom makes us sound like Beyoncé and which room makes us sound like a dying cat. So in God's house, I imagine the layout, the choice of materials, all of it, was picked out for the choir of the Judaic temple. After all, Solomon was given great wisdom - but that was after Asaph.

This choir was led, at one point, by Asaph. This excites me. Was he the first worship leader? Could it be? If I were a worship leader, I would be pouring over the psalms of Asaph and his life. Asaph is listed as a chief of the Levites (selected tribe). He is also said to be prophetic. Sounds like someone we should be paying attention to.

His position alone doesn't mean much. We know that there were plenty of Levites that dishonored God and their position. We know plenty of priests throughout the Old Testament that God wanted nothing to do with, and not that long before Asaph! However, Asaph was not in that crowd. He was over the use of the instruments within the temple. As we can see, he is credited with writing his fair share of Psalms.

Some historians believe that Asaph's job may have also included writing down the psalms of David- A recorder of sorts. These historians also feel that the psalms listed under his name were simply David's written down by Asaph. I find this difficult to swallow. Looking through various translations you see plain and simple "Of David" or "Of Solomon" and now "Of Asaph." I can see how Asaph would take on the job of writing down the psalms of David. It seems fitting for the choir director in the temple of God to keep a record of songs of praise. I, however, believe what most believe when they go through the history - Asaph knew how to write songs too.

Asaph was a priest by lineage and a prophet as any was - by gift and grace of God. He was a worshipper, song writer, and choir master, by choice. Now, he did not elect himself as the one in charge. David appointed him to the position. However, he had the option, like every priest before and after him, to follow God or act evil. Each king and priest is listed as doing what was right in the eyes of the Lord or evil. Just as you and I have a choice to be for God or against him. With God, there is no in between. You are either for or against. End of story. Asaph chose for. In the story of Asaph we see that his sons were also in the priestly ministry. They were part of his choir, as were his brothers. And after Asaph was finished, his son took over. As a parent I can say, there is nothing better than when a child steps into their own faith and does not rely on yours. Asaph was a husband and father who raised children to follow the Lord.

When it comes to the writings of scripture, there are many times that we decide that we need to take the teachings from credible sources. The gospels are written by those that were right with Jesus. The letters were written by the ultimate convert, mostly from prison. So this Asaph needs a back story, or so we think. Where do we first learn of Asaph? In First Chronicles, we are introduced to Asaph and his family. David has decided to bring back the Ark of the Covenant to the holy city. The last time this was attempted the Israelites failed miserably. The ark was placed on a cart. It began to slide. The closest person to it reached out to steady it. They died on the spot. God has had the same rules from the beginning. So David, knowing God's heart, sets up the delivery of the ark the correct way. He brings out the Levites - the only ones deemed appropriate by God to handle the ark. Then he lines everything up. Everyone has a job. Certain men are in charge of transporting the ark. Others are in charge of worship before the ark. Enter Asaph - 1 Chronicles 16. His job is to lead Israel in thanksgiving as the ark is brought back to the city. Then David left Asaph and his relatives before the ark of the covenant of the Lord to minister before the ark continually.

All of that means a little here and there that adds up to more. Asaph made the right choice even when things were hard. He wrote psalms that expressed his true emotions, not just what he thinks God wants of him. When I read Psalm 77, I hear pain. I hear a man doing what he can and realizing, as Isaiah will restate generations later, that God's way is not our way. We're human. We choose dry land, clear paths, and easy ways. But Asaph stands on the shore and sees God walking through the seas and storms- and he follows.

Through the good and the bad, Asaph knows where to turn. He knows that God is still in control. He lifts his voice to the Alpha and Omega knowing that he won't always see God's steps, but the path is still there before him. He needs faith. He knows that stepping in the storm is better than standing on the shore. Asaph echoes the cries of David, his king, to show him the way and take him through the storm. Immediately after Asaph says that God's footsteps are unseen he tells us:

> You led your people like a flock By the hand of Moses and Aaron.

> Asaph knows God will lead.

The Hail Mary Throw
Chapter 16

Not long ago my car decided it didn't enjoy being a functioning car. Oh terrible. Panic set in. Then I tried the over spiritual, "God, I need a miracle..." prayer. Yeah, I had a feeling God was going to giggle through that one. And after some more time I did what I always try to do - muscle it. Well, I broke something else and smashed my elbow into the middle console. Yup, I'm a classy lady.

Once the tow truck hauled ole Babs off, my mother had rescued the kids to take them home to change for ballet and my husband retrieved me to head to the mechanic, I was able to sit back and register it all. The wish-on-a-star, miracle prayer was gone. It was time to be real. The mechanic was going to call and let me know the issue later on. My husband took me home with enough time to take the kids to ballet himself. I sat and said, "Now what do I do?" My husband then told me what I wanted and needed to hear. "You're going to go for a run and kick this stuff out." He knew my mind and body needed to hit reset. Ctl + alt + del. Reboot.

Truthfully, I didn't want to run. I wanted to curl up in a ball on my bed and sleep. My body and mind wanted rebellion. But deep inside I knew that I needed to get out and run. Running destresses me. Physically, my body needed to let out the tension. It was a run or boxing. Mentally, I needed the movement and fresh air. Spiritually, I needed to keep the distractions of the world far enough away to draw closer to God.

Off I went. Within the first half mile my body was still longing to curl up in the fetal position. But my heart was opening up to God in the midst of truth and reality. Up until then I was feeling numb. We had just set our budget up for the month and were feeling good. We took our tax refund and paid bills. We were winning financially. Now my car is looking like we shouldn't have paid those doctors' bills in full. Numb. Lost. I paid the $80 to tow my car and was left waiting for the diagnosis from the mechanic. But as I ran, I spoke the most honest words I knew. "God, you always provide. I don't know why I worry. It's always in your hands and somehow we make it out okay. You'll provide what we need."

After that I didn't think much of the situation. I eagerly awaited a call that didn't come. By the time I

Together
Chapter 17

When I set out to write this, I was so enamored by the psalm. I read it over and over again focusing on verse 19. For a while I couldn't figure out what it was about this psalm and verse I find so infectious. Then I figured out what it is - Hope.

This may not look like a passage of hope, but it is to me. Everywhere in life we see imbalances, injustices, and climbing up, or falling down, ladders. Those born to certain classes (be it social, economical, or racial) get the short end of the stick or the silver spoon in their mouth. Here in America we hear that everyone has the same opportunities, but that isn't the case. This passage levels the playing field in my eyes.

It is another cry for God to rescue, but also shows us what we must do. It doesn't say that certain people have to work a certain way. We don't get to bypass storms of life based on pedigree or upbringing. Isn't that a reason to hope? You may look on this as a reason to despair, but we're all doomed to suffer through storms and pain. We will all struggle to see God's steps to walk in.

There is something to be said about the camaraderie of being a struggling human being. We've all experienced a time of storms. As a culture through the last few generations, we were told to weather the storm alone. Our struggles are our own. Galatians 6 tells us to carry each other's loads. That means in order to receive help, we need to open up about our struggles and pains.

When I was in college, a book was released that brought men into community groups. Many, young and old alike, flocked to these groups for accountability. What was supposed to be sharing to ask for help, seek encouragement, and be held accountable ended up turning into people spilling their secrets, feeling lifted up, but not turning away from sin that entangled them. The idea was meant to dispel sin and bear one another's burdens. I truly wish more accountability groups had been more than just sharing sin. However, communities did in fact grow again.

The popularity of accountability groups stemmed from the fact that people want to get off their chests the wrong they've done without the judgment that so many church atmospheres have brought. Unfortunately, there was

Headphones or Speakers?
Chapter 18

Throughout this book, as I've written, I have faced some oppositions. Like what? Oh, thanks for asking. For one, the constant struggle for me is finding the time to write. I know many would probably think that ridiculous, but it's true. I have things that "must" be done. If I have a client, and we have an appointment, I need to be there. I also have these smallish creatures that depend on me for things like food, clean clothes, and a clean house. I, like so many others, have responsibilities. If I do not take care of my responsibilities, other people, that I care about, suffer. So what are my options? I can wake up earlier and write - hmm before 4:45 and functioning enough for complete thoughts, maybe not. Or I do my writing after my responsibilities are taken care of and I can sneak it in between duties of life. That is typically what happens. Though, some days, it is hard to write about God's path or any God-centered- thoughts when the day has not gone well. In fact, some days I wish I could just take a nap and watch TV. But this is what I have been called to, so this is what I do. I'm also old school and prefer pen and paper. Typing my work is my first round of edits, but it makes the entire process longer. So after a while, I hit a wall with this book. My fear and doubt settled within me. I couldn't just walk away though. I knew God had me on this path for a reason, so I kept walking. Since I didn't have direction - words- I started typing. As of the first draft of this sentence I have the first eleven chapters typed. I began to wonder if I would simply catch up and have nothing else to write when I heard God's voice.

Interesting isn't it? That phrase we use to "hearing God's voice." I wish it was audible, but of course, it is not. But we do "hear" him, don't we? Don't you? That's what God wanted me to focus on. This isn't about the voice of God or interpreting his words. None of this can happen, nor does it matter without one clear point.

You must have a relationship with God. So often I write these books or blog posts and just assume that we're all on the same page. We aren't. I know that within the church we have a variety of denominations with different beliefs. I read a book by a pastor that said he followed Christ for over a decade before he finally heard God speaking to him. I wanted to put the book down and walk away. My mind started racing with, "Then you weren't saved all that long ago." And, "You didn't know to listen or what you were listening to!" But I continued to read because I had already been so invested in the author and book. So as I read, it did actually fall into my second thought. He was waiting for the booming voice. He then discovered how God had been speaking to him the whole time through Scripture and the Holy Spirit and he just didn't connect. When you give your life to God, you don't say a prayer and walk away. You then make choices each day to honor him. It isn't a following like a cult, it is a relationship. We don't do good and avoid bad out of fear of wrath or hope of blessing. We act out of love.

That relationship of Father and child motivates us to move and grow in ways that fear of punishment cannot. We don't do because we have to. We do because we want to. We have that connection. The desire is also because we have a two-way connection.

We have had relationships in this world that are filled with love. It could be a parental/child love, a brotherly love, or a romantic love. I can bet that out of those three, you have had at least one time where the relationship was one-sided. When we give, give, give, and never receive love, we are in a one-sided relationship. Then we are drained. However, if the relationship has both people contributing, we have a different story. Love reciprocated is unstoppable.

When we (the sinners that broke the relationship) turn and love God, we are now reciprocating the love that God has been giving all along. The difference between what I described in the previous paragraph and this situation is that God will not be drained. He will not run out of love for us.

In fact, when we turn to him, we now have access to the path we need to take. It only comes through our repentance, our turn from fleshly living to God and what he has called us to do. The reason for one sided relationships with God is us, not Him. We see how God gives to us and yet we keep asking for more. When bad things happen we blame God, not sin. When good things happen we claim luck, not blessing. To change all of this, we need a relationship with Him. So many say a prayer to "ask Jesus into their hearts," but too many do nothing from there. In order to find the path, we need to know the one who creates the path.

The relationship with God helps us, not him. He's God. He owns the cattle on a thousand hills. He is omniscient, omnipresent, and omnipotent. He gave us free will, not the other way around. And from the beginning, he chose us. He wants us. It begins in a one-sided relationship from our birth. He gives us life. He shows us how to find him. He speaks to us, but it is only when we go to him that we truly listen. We speak to him not as the god that gave us bad luck, but as the God that gives what we need, as a Father to us.

Our relationship with him guides us through the choppy waves. He starts us in the shallows as we learn to feel the undertow and understand how sand will move beneath our feet if we are still. He calls to us during calm and storm. We learn to hear his voice. We learn to follow in the big steps. We read the Bible, pray, and glean from others. And then we walk. Nowhere in our relationship should we go back to one sided. We don't sit on the beach and work on our tan while others go through the deep.

A call to walk the deep is a call to faith. We need to live a life that requires faith. If we believe we can do it all, then we don't need God. Walking the deep takes faith. We must know that God is there providing a path that we don't see. We need to also believe that God is there with us in the deep. That is faith.

When I was teaching my son to swim we went through trying times. He would cry and scream clinging to me. Time and time again we would practice. Typically by the end, we would make progress, but the next day would start the same. Then one day, as he cried and wailed, I held him. He was terrified of drowning, though I was never out of reach. So I held him. Finally, he calmed down. I asked him if he thought I loved him... He said he did. So I asked him if he believed that I love him. He said, "Isn't that the same thing?" So I told him that I thought with my mind, but I believed with my heart and my mind. As he pondered, I asked him again if he believed that I loved him. He did, or said he did. So I asked him, "If I love you the way I do, and you believe that I love you that much, would I try to hurt you?" By now you see where this is going. He didn't trust himself in the water. He didn't trust the water. He trusted me, guiding him in his swim lessons to want the best for him. He now loves to swim. He knows to have a rational fear of himself in the water, but to trust that he can swim or that I'll be there to get him when he struggles.

Do you trust and believe?

Jump!
Chapter 19

It has been some time since I took my children to the beach as a South Carolinian should. Last year my family made an attempt while vacationing in Boca Raton, Florida and only needing to walk across the street. But it has been years since I've driven 45 minutes to the beach in South Carolina. So now that the kids are older, I feel okay taking them without my husband to man one while I watch the other. Taking the kids was a chance to broaden our areas of travel during school and work hours. And it did in fact do that.

Before we left the coastline, I sat in the chair watching my two in the water. God whispered to me and my mind began to race. I didn't bring my writing because I didn't want it to get all sandy. I couldn't wait to get home and get to work on what God revealed to me.

I had spent over an hour watching my children at the shoreline. I found the water too cold, but kids have a tolerance for cold water when fun is involved. I allowed them to enter without me as long as they followed the rules I gave them. When I was a child I liked to move with the waves. My children, however, prefer to attempt to jump over the waves as they roll in.

They held hands, jumped, and laughed. Sometimes they fell, but typically they landed on their feet. One time my daughter fell and a wave caught her in the face before she could get on her feet. She came running out of the water to me. I helped her get her towel and dry her face. She was ready to run back, but I had to stop her. "Anything near your belly," I advised, "just stand still and let the wave hit you. If you jump at those higher ones it will take your feet out and you'll fall." She barely acknowledged that she heard me before running back to her brother.

Back at it they went. And for the most part, she heeded my advice. But every once in a while, she jumped when she should have stayed put. She didn't whine or complain. She would run out, wipe her face and keep going. It wasn't until after two hours of watching them that God opened my eyes to what I was really seeing.

Here I am writing about the ocean we are to walk through and watching littles. Duh! Here's the quick point: When our feet stay grounded in the big waves, we don't get knocked down. But here is the hard part - keeping our feet firm is not fun. Jumping over is the fun part.

Even after an hour of being at the beach, my daughter didn't always take my advice. Why? She knew what I was saying was true. She didn't care if her face got wet. All that mattered was that she had more fun. Jumping, for a four year old, is so much more fun than standing still.

Do you know what else is typically fun? Sin. Sin is fun, well, if you're doing it right. If sin was not fun, we would have no problem leaving it behind to stand firm.

It was such a beautiful and simple picture from God. We are God's children. As he leads us through the depths of the ocean and we get ourselves caught in this storm we need a sure foot. When we are steadied (in shoes of the gospel of peace) we can let the waves come at us and stand. When we jump and have fun, the wave tumbles us around. We get a little mixed up and turned around. It takes more time to get back on the course that we were on, rather than just standing and maybe being pushed back before continuing on.

As I saw my children, I felt like I understood God if only for a moment. Every time my daughter was knocked down, I worried. I worried over the next wave that was coming at her. The new wave that would hit her face, get swallowed inadvertently, and blur her vision. I think of God saying, "I told you not to jump...Oh get up. Get up!...

~ 113 ~

Watch the next wave!" How great it is that God does not experience the exhaustion that we do? But here we are, feeble humans. A fun wave comes and we jump. Down we go- got drunk at a party, cussed out the driver ahead of us, cheated on a test. One wave swept our feet out from under us. The second covered us - getting drunk every weekend, cussing for the fun of it, cheating on a spouse. Over and over God is saying, "Get up."

What was beautiful in all of this was that God was showing me an additional piece to the puzzle. As the church, we should be there for one another, picking others out of their sin, and helping them hold on when the next wave comes. My son was doing that for my daughter. Each time she went down, he was at her side. His hand was down to scoop her up. His head was up checking for the next wave that might hit her. He was ready to protect her. I was there as well. Every time her face was covered, I had her towel read for her to wipe. She didn't care for the saltwater in her eye. We experience that. We sin, and then we don't like it. We run back to the shore and clean ourselves up - repentance- and go back to the waves.

The problem I see is that we don't have enough people acting as my son did. We have many willing to walk into the ocean with their younger Christian siblings. We will pull people up. We will check on them. Then what happens? We judge. We nudge. We nag. I am not

Think back to this time again. Stories, their history, are passed down through generations mostly through word of mouth as well as by a few writers. We had slaves in America (legally, unfortunately) until 1863. Fewer than 400 years have passed on this soil and yet younger generations seem to miss it. With textbooks, internet, public and private education, kids take it all for granted. For example, my son and I were covering Dr. Martin Luther King Jr. We were discussing his famous "I Have a Dream" speech. My son took down the year in his notebook, but didn't grasp it until I asked him how long ago it was. After doing the math, he realized that all of his grandparents had been alive for the speech. It was in that moment that he comprehended that it was not that long ago after all.

Why do I give this example? Well, here in America, we figure things must have been forever ago. I feel that way when I think of how long ago it was that indoor plumbing was expected in homes. My mind doesn't want to think about grandparents and outhouses. With a rapid growth in technology, we seem to forget the past faster and faster. It wasn't that way for King David and his people. They were taught to remember the stories of God and Israel. And it is that foundation of faithfulness that Asaph draws upon at the end of Psalm 77.

Asaph goes back to God's faithfulness in his time of despair. He says that God's people are led like a flock. It's interesting that this is the choice Jesus uses so often as well. A flock of sheep is something mundane for the average American. Not many of us are in the business of sheep herding. I was able to watch an interesting video, however, about a shepherd and his sheep. The shepherd had allowed a group to visit his fields. The sheep were out grazing. Person after person attempted the shepherd's call to get the sheep to them. Person after person fails. One person was able to get a sheep or two to look over, but that was about it. Then the shepherd called and the field of grass eaters came running to him. The flock knows the shepherd's voice. That is the point Jesus made over and over again. In order to be led through the storms and deep of the ocean, we have to know how to listen to God's voice.

But what he says next is wonderful as well. "By the hand of Moses and Aaron." During the Old Testament days, the Holy Spirit wasn't given to those who believed. Instead, they had the Tabernacle where the presence of God dwelled. When the Israelites left Egypt they followed Moses, who was being led by God. There was always a fire at night and a pillar of smoke during the day. Can you just imagine that? Literally following the fire and smoke of God? No questions there. And Moses and Aaron knew where to go because God spoke to them. They told the Levites where to walk.

Now picture Asaph. He is there when David orders the Ark to be brought back to God's people. He leads the songs of thanksgiving. Don't you think he hopes for the days of Moses and Aaron, just a bit? Times are becoming harder. Waves are crashing. He remembers the stories of his father's fathers. Maybe he thinks it unfair, in a state of jealousy, that the Israelites before him were led in direct smoke and fire, and here they are rescuing the same ark that Saul had lost before. Insert the stomping of feet. "Where are you, God?" he cries in pain.

See, I feel very connected to him here. Spending my life with the church means I have spent most of my life hearing the Word of God, his promises and the truth. Time after time I get frustrated. Okay, let's say agitated. No, honesty pushes me. I get angry. I do the best I can with the life I have been given. I'm always striving to do better. And, yet, there are still times I feel abandoned by God. I feel the push of the current dragging me off course and I ask God, "Will the Lord reject me forever? Will you keep your favor from me? Hey, God! Do you remember me? Do you see me?" No sooner have I finished my whining before the words I've heard and read for decades fill my mind. And by the hands of countless godly influences, I'm brought back to the truth.

Asaph knows this truth. God is the same yesterday, today, and forever. He does not break his promises. If he says that he will lead us through the storm, he will. He is the steady rock. We are the ones that waver. Asaph goes back to what he knows, by the hands of Moses and Aaron, Israel made it through the storms. They made it through by following God.

You may think it's slightly egotistical to promote the hands of men rather than the hands of God. I would ask if you remember the battles. One in particular in Exodus 17 stands out. In this battle, Joshua was leading the Israelites against Amalek. The Lord told Moses that as long as his hands were raised, they would win the battle. So Moses, Aaron, and Hur headed up to a hill and watch. Just as God said, when Moses' arms are raised, Israel gained control. But Moses was a man. Men get tired. As he became weary, his arms dropped and Israel fell a bit. So Aaron and Hur used a rock and their own strength to keep Moses' arms raised until Joshua defeated Amalek.

Who won the battle? God. Who got the credit? God. Who had a job to do? Moses, Aaron, Hur, Joshua, and Israel. The same is always true of us. The war is won. God wins. But we still have to do the work and enter the battle. By Moses' arms being raised, the battle was won. After Moses, Aaron took over the leadership of Israel and, by his hands, Israel was led into the promise land.

Approaching the path has become different for me as well. I think many people can attest to the different ways we can attempt the path God has for us.

First, I think, many choose to sit and wait for the directions. People sit around and wait for the booming voice or some big sign from God that tells them where to go and what to do. This leads to two areas of problems. The first is that too many sit so long that they don't remember who and what they are waiting for. Or they just refuse to move. Their life is nothing more than sitting and waiting. Never moving. The second issue that arises is that many wait for so long that they assume any voice or billboard is what they need. They then move in a direction just to move, not guided by God. Which leads us to the next attempt.

Second, people just start moving! They give their lives to Christ and head off to the crusades. Typically these people will go and do because God is moving. If God is moving in the inner cities, so are they. If God is moving in Haiti, so are they. If God is moving in local churches, so are they. These people usually don't recognize that there are specific callings for each of us as well as our church-wide calling of making disciples of all nations. These people are too anxious to sit still.

Third, I see people that step out into the waves knowing it's going to be a little rocky at fist. They are cautious and maybe hesitant, but still move forward. Then as time goes on, they hit the bigger waves, storms, wind, and things get harder. When things were difficult in the beginning, it was a learning curve. But things getting harder? That sometimes wasn't in the person's plans so they get bitter and angry. Then they quit. They take their own path thinking God wasn't in the deep waves and storm clouds.

Finally, we end up with the seasoned path finders. There are many that grow up and change a bit. Perhaps they started as one of the first three or a combination of them. As time goes on, they have to make choices. Do the waiters enter the water? Do the runarounds find the steady gait? Do the bitter find truth?

Like I said, I've learned. I've had times of working on my tan. Sure I was on the sand. I searched the waves only to come up with nothing. So I followed others, but it wasn't my path. I walk slowly, steadily, and purposefully. And I can look back at my past to know my tendencies. So when I want to head back to shore, I know better.

I know that sometimes the life lessons and methods of path following take a few more trial and errors than others. I know that some people need more work than others. Some, like me, are hard wired to be stubborn. Many let pride carry them away. Just as Adam and Eve gave way to the lie of the serpent, we too believe we know what's best for ourselves. It is so difficult to give up ourselves.

Jesus tells us that if we want to truly live our lives we have to lose them. That's what walking the unseen path is. We give up our way- safe, comfortable, easy- and turn to God's. Even though we can't see the path, He can. He knows where he is going, what he is doing, and where he is leading. God, in his omniscience, knows that we will make mistakes. He knows that we will mess up on our way to finding his path and that we won't always follow properly. That's where his grace is. His grace allows us to put down our lives, take up his cross, and follow. And every stupid time we put down our cross he shows grace. That is why Christ tells us to do it daily. If we wake up and can thank him for another chance, we can start each day fresh. We put down our own ideas and take up his.

Following Him is the most difficult thing to do some times. Other times it is as easy as counting to ten. Either way it is the single most rewarding path one can take. Not even the idea of heaven. Not even the eternity in God's presence and seeing his face. The reward of the path is walking with God right here. It's coming alongside others and having others come alongside you. It's helping the needy, feeding the poor, sitting with the lonely. It is watching children be innocent and knowing that this is what God had wanted for us. It's living a life that is meaningful and purposeful. Jesus said he came so that we can have life and have it to the fullest capacity. And that is our reward. (Though I am not knocking spending eternity with God! I cannot wait to look upon his face. To fully know as I am fully known.)

Throughout it all, we must continue to focus on the cross. When we live our lives reminded of the ultimate price paid for us, we keep perspective. It's easier to follow someone that has loved us deeper than anyone else has than to follow the god in the box that so many unbelievers think they know. We move in love. Not our love, but his love first and foremost. Then, we walk in both his love and our love attempting to reciprocate. We fix our eyes on the cross and humble ourselves to carry our own cross each day. We recognize our path has in fact been walked before. We don't walk it because it's been done before so obviously we can do it too. No! We humbly say that God walked it and He is with us as we walk it and that is why we can.

The unseen path is there for us to take. It will be the toughest path there is. And as the days go on, we appreciate the challenge as it draws us closer to God. The path will lead to growth. The path will refine. The path we cannot see, will bring us into his glory.

Acknowledgements

A big thank you to my family for allowing me the time to write and put words to paper when needed. There is understanding that pours from you that people cannot comprehend.

Thank you to Jon Davis, a godly man that encourages his sheep and gives wisdom freely. Without his constant teaching, I would be blind to many things of the Word of God.

Finally, thank you to the friends that push me to write continually and share the words that God gives me. Thank you for letting me bounce ideas off you constantly.

About the Author

Jewel Sweeney is a wife and mother residing in South Carolina. She is the author of several works ranging in a wide variety of genres. Jewel believes there are times for encouragement and challenge, but also a time for fun and laughter. The spices of life season her writing styles. She is the author of a children's series titled *The Adventures of Bugaboo & Ladybug.* Her non-fiction works include *A Time to Walk, Running 101,* and *Conditioning 201.*

60670485R00086

Made in the USA
Columbia, SC
20 June 2019